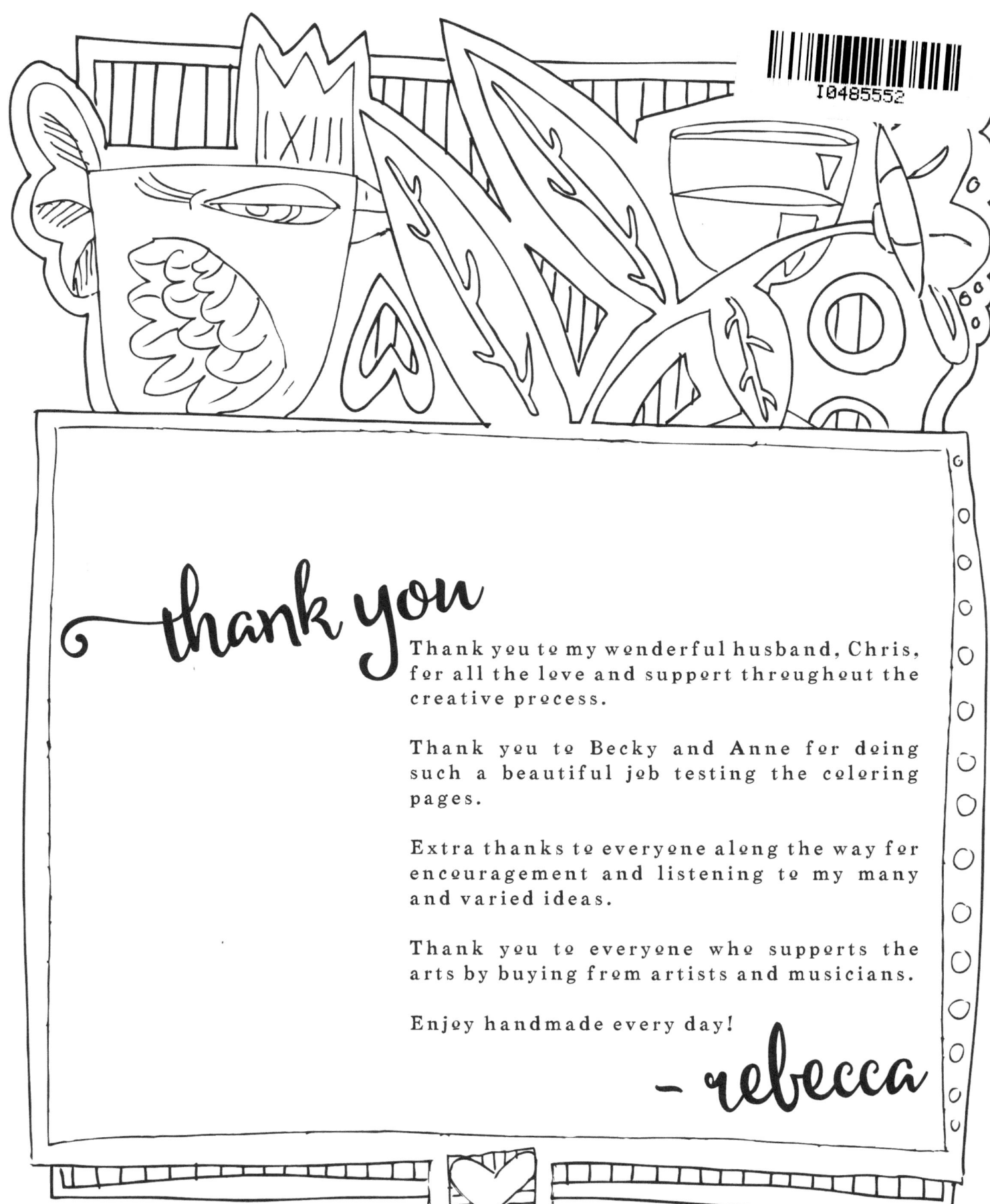

thank you

Thank you to my wonderful husband, Chris, for all the love and support throughout the creative process.

Thank you to Becky and Anne for doing such a beautiful job testing the coloring pages.

Extra thanks to everyone along the way for encouragement and listening to my many and varied ideas.

Thank you to everyone who supports the arts by buying from artists and musicians.

Enjoy handmade every day!

— rebecca

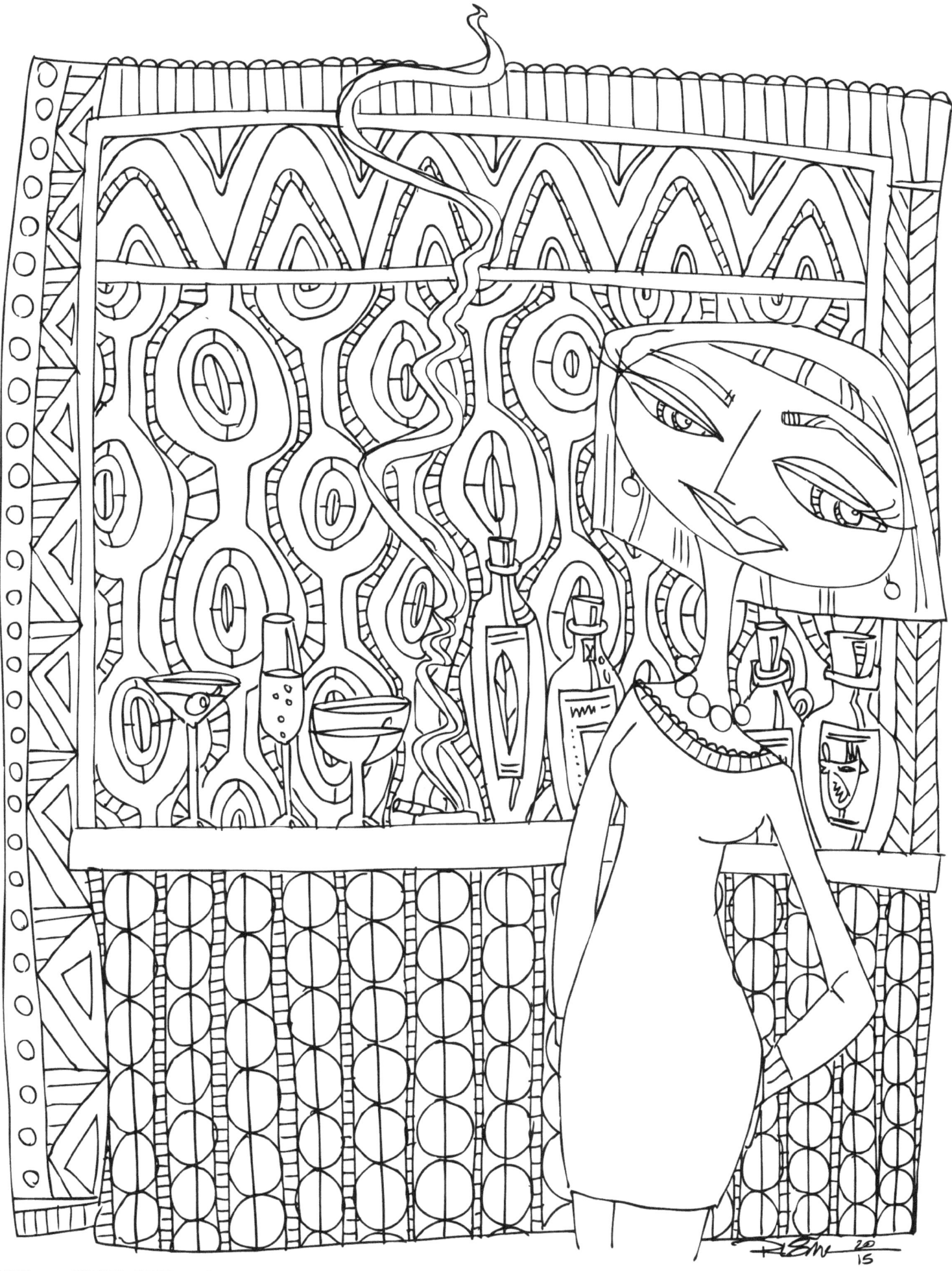

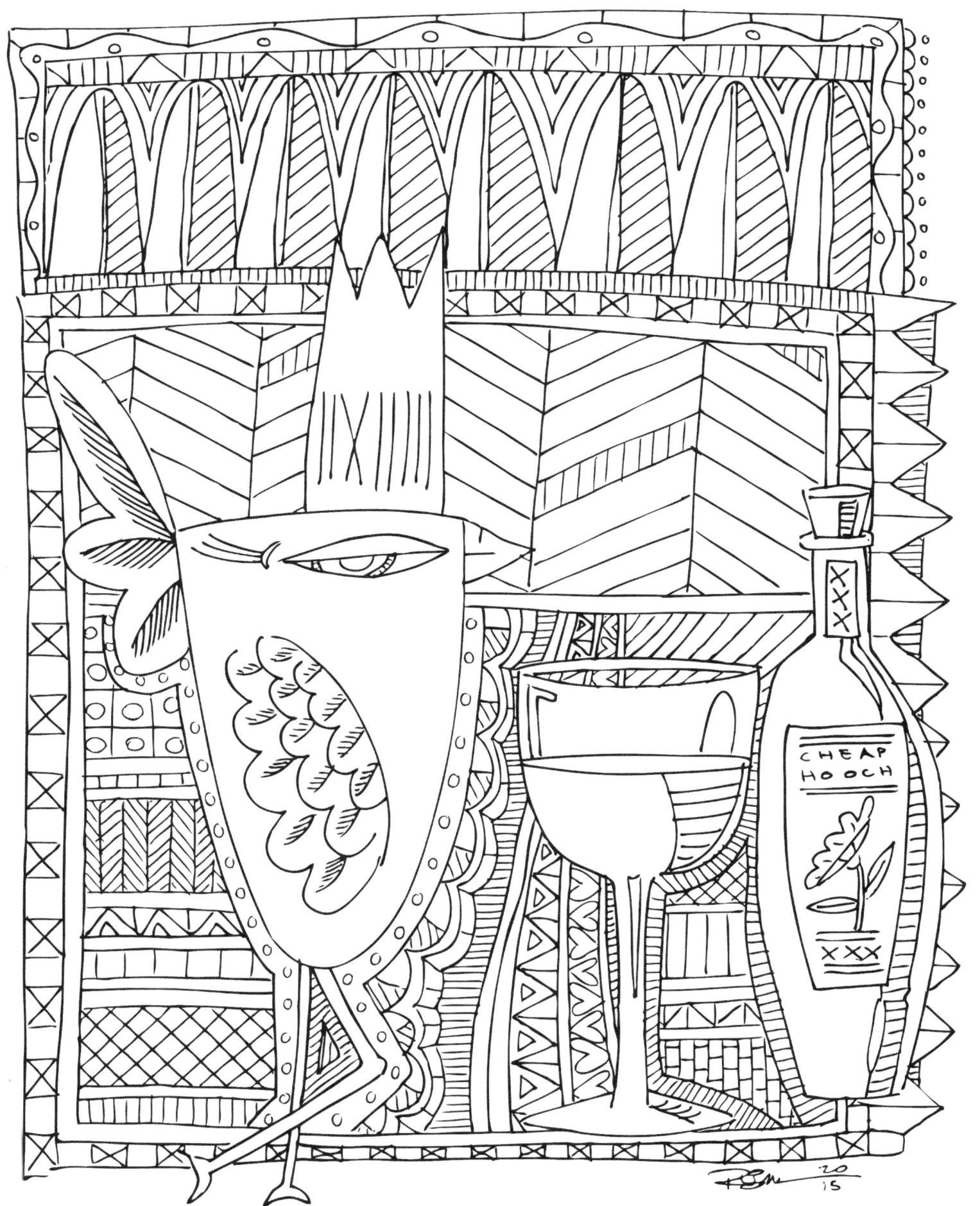

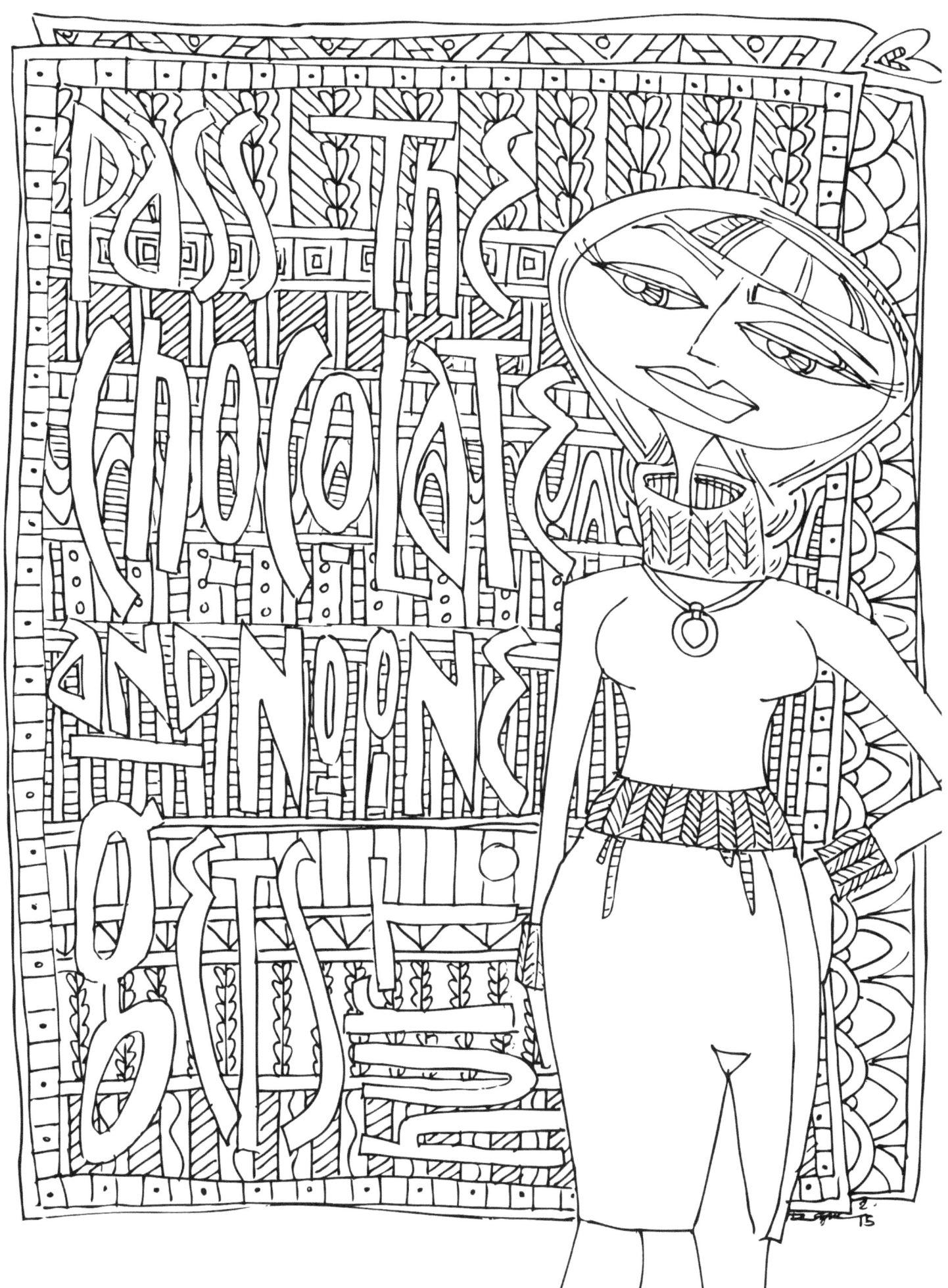

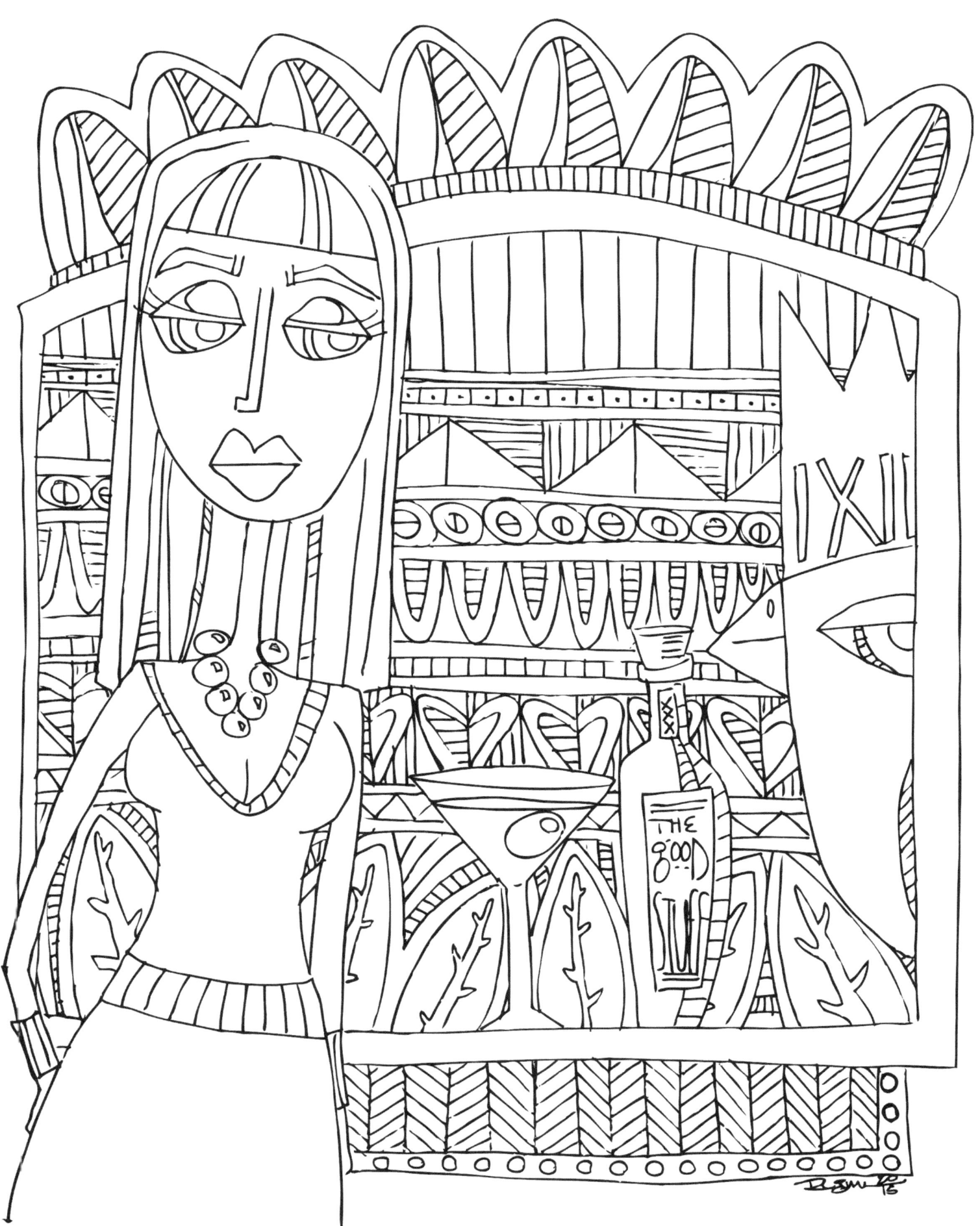

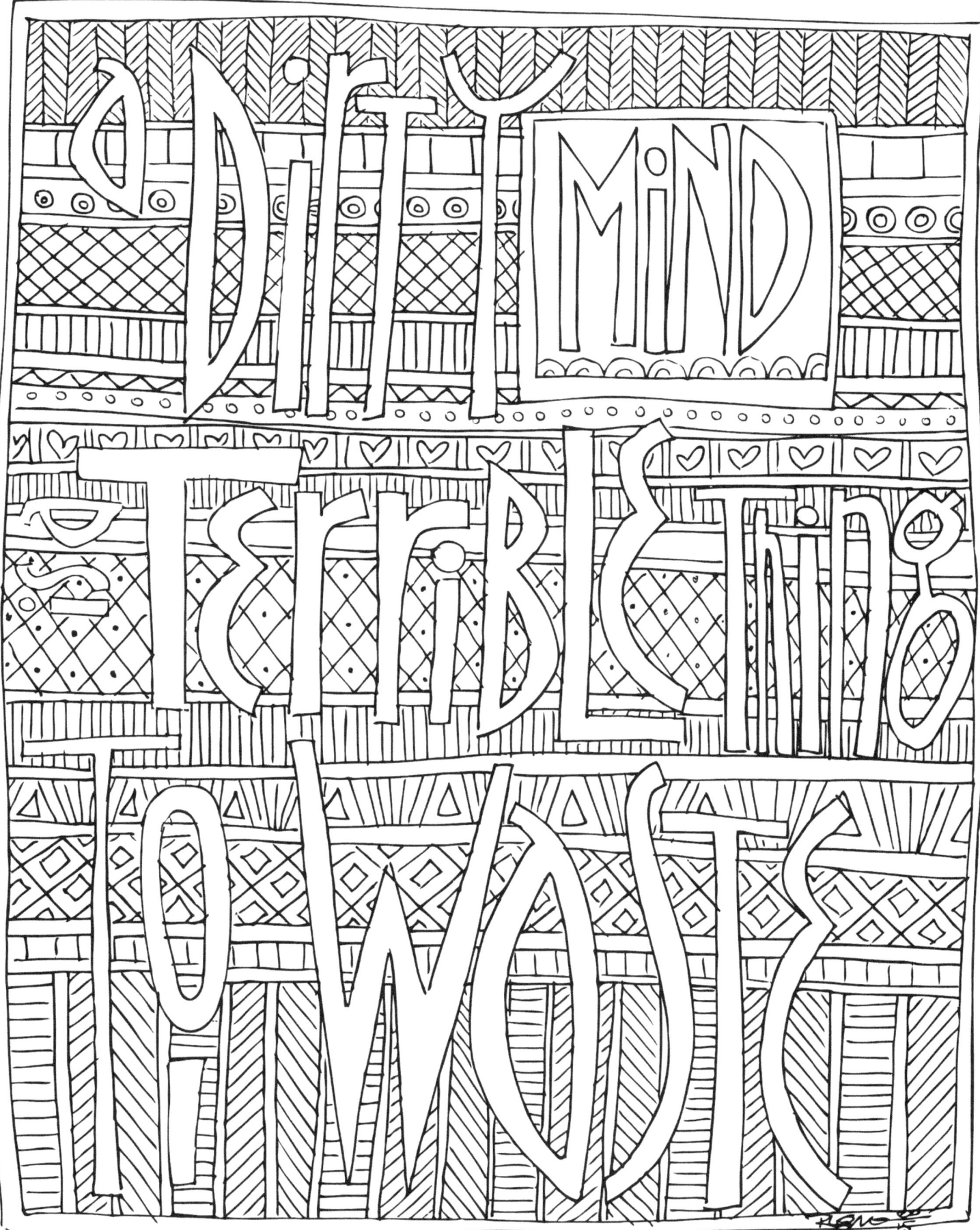

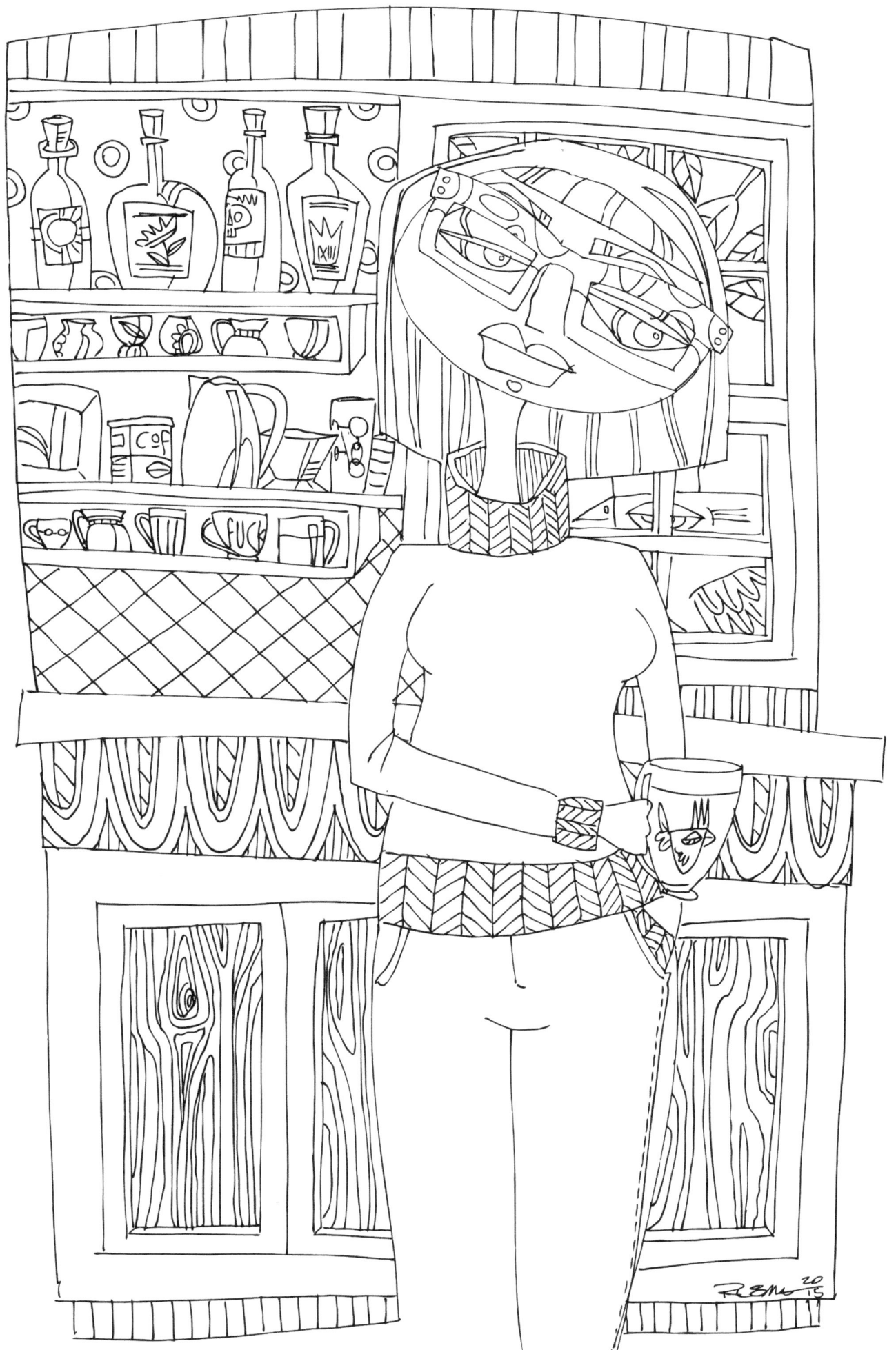

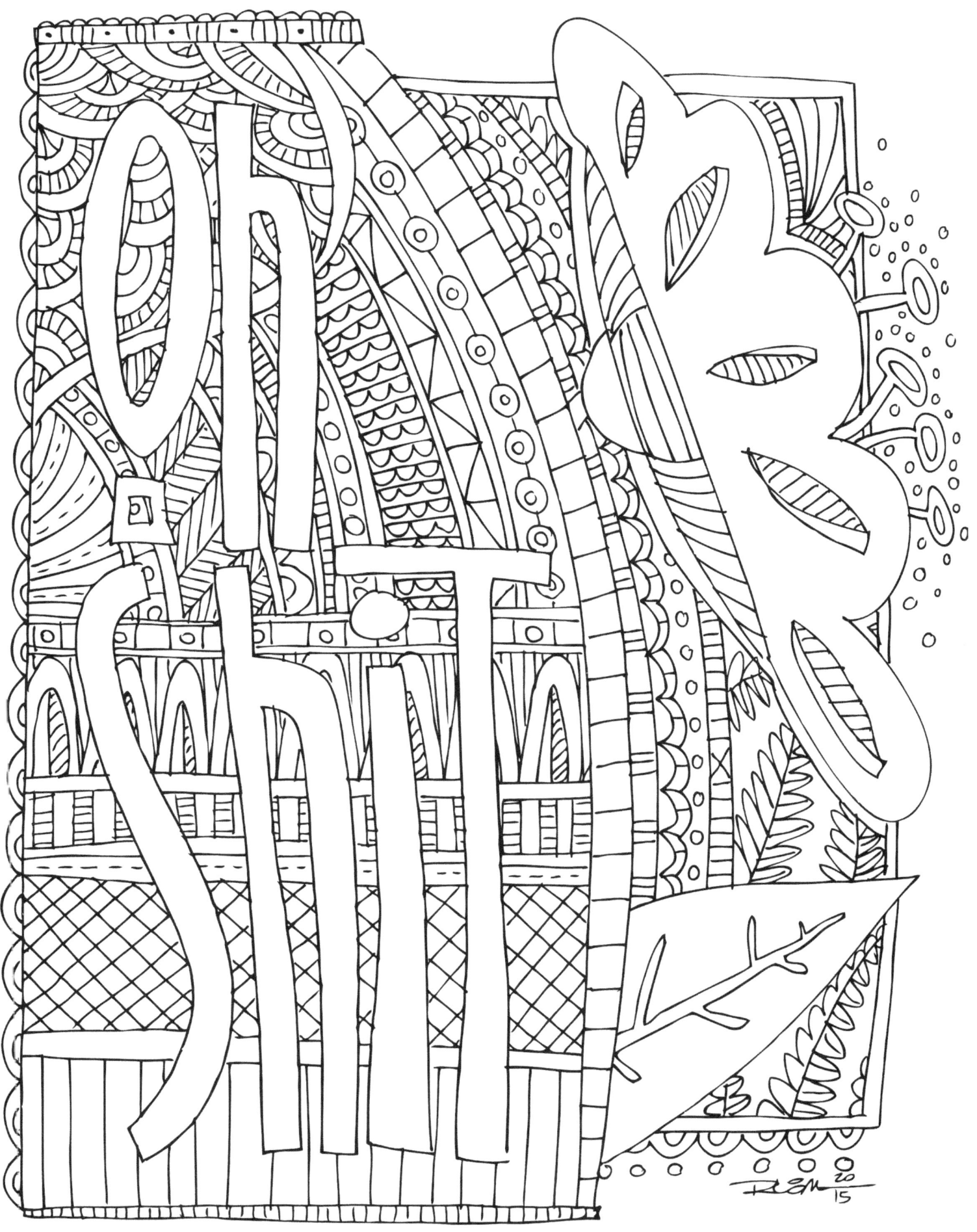

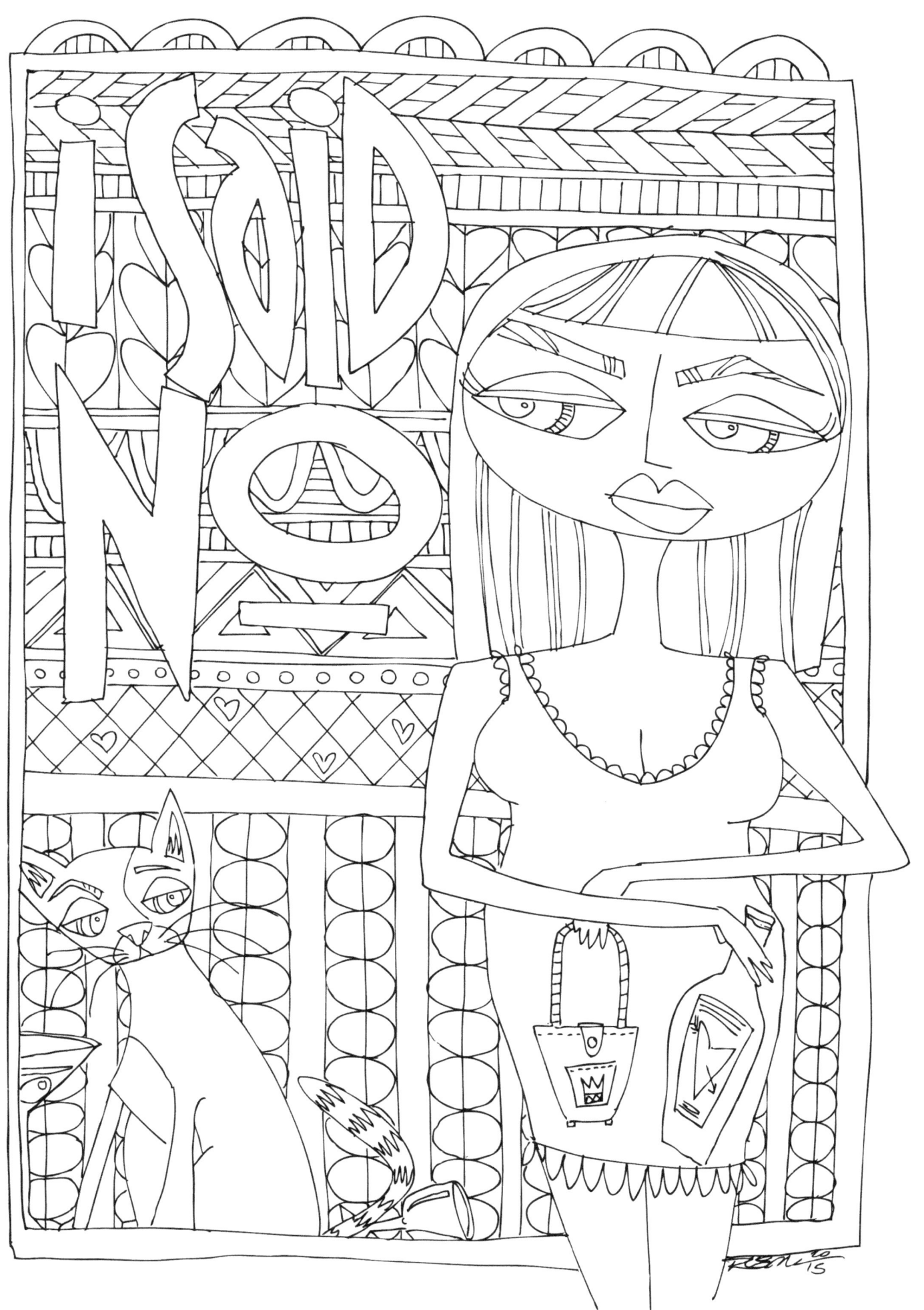

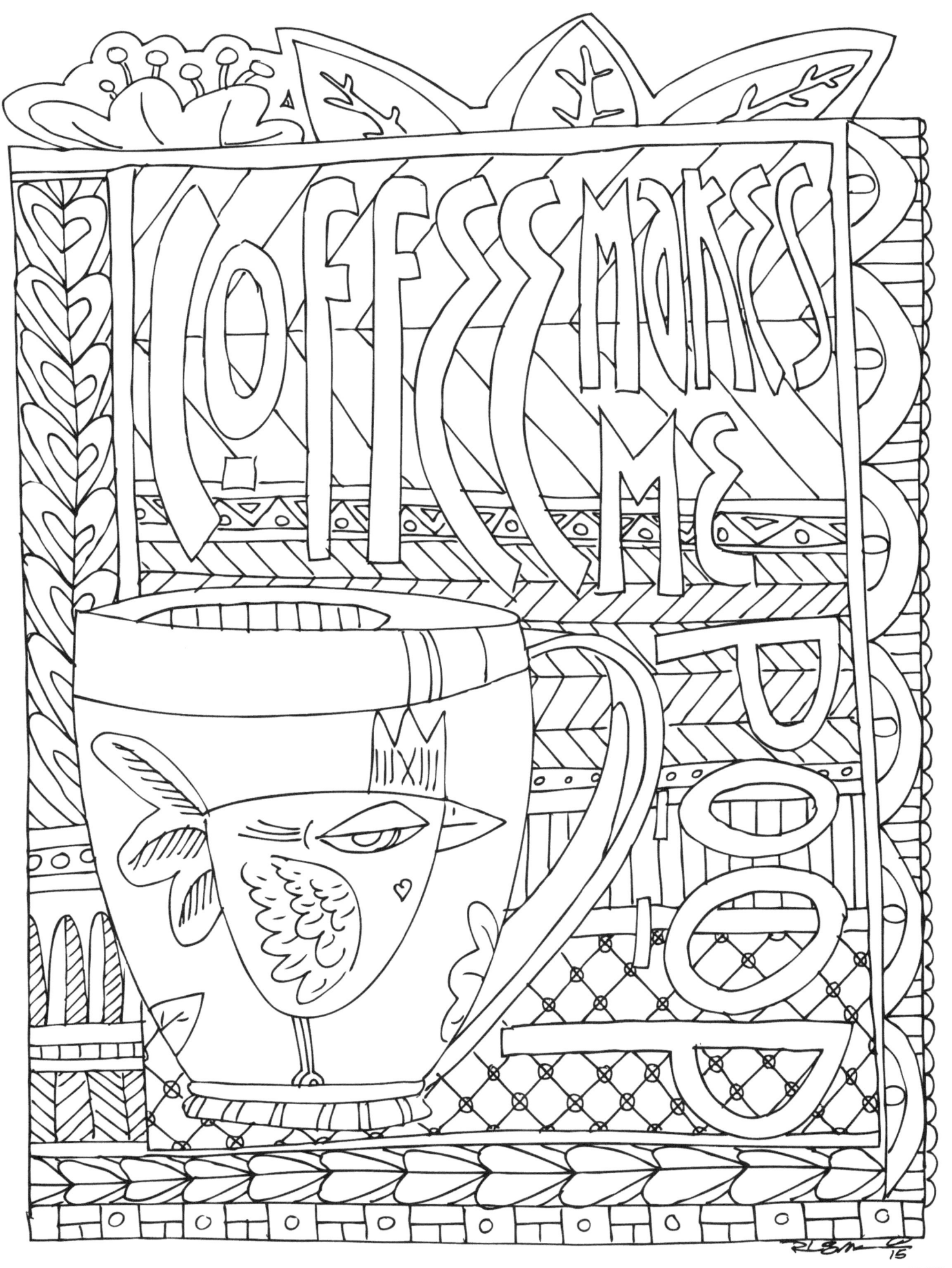

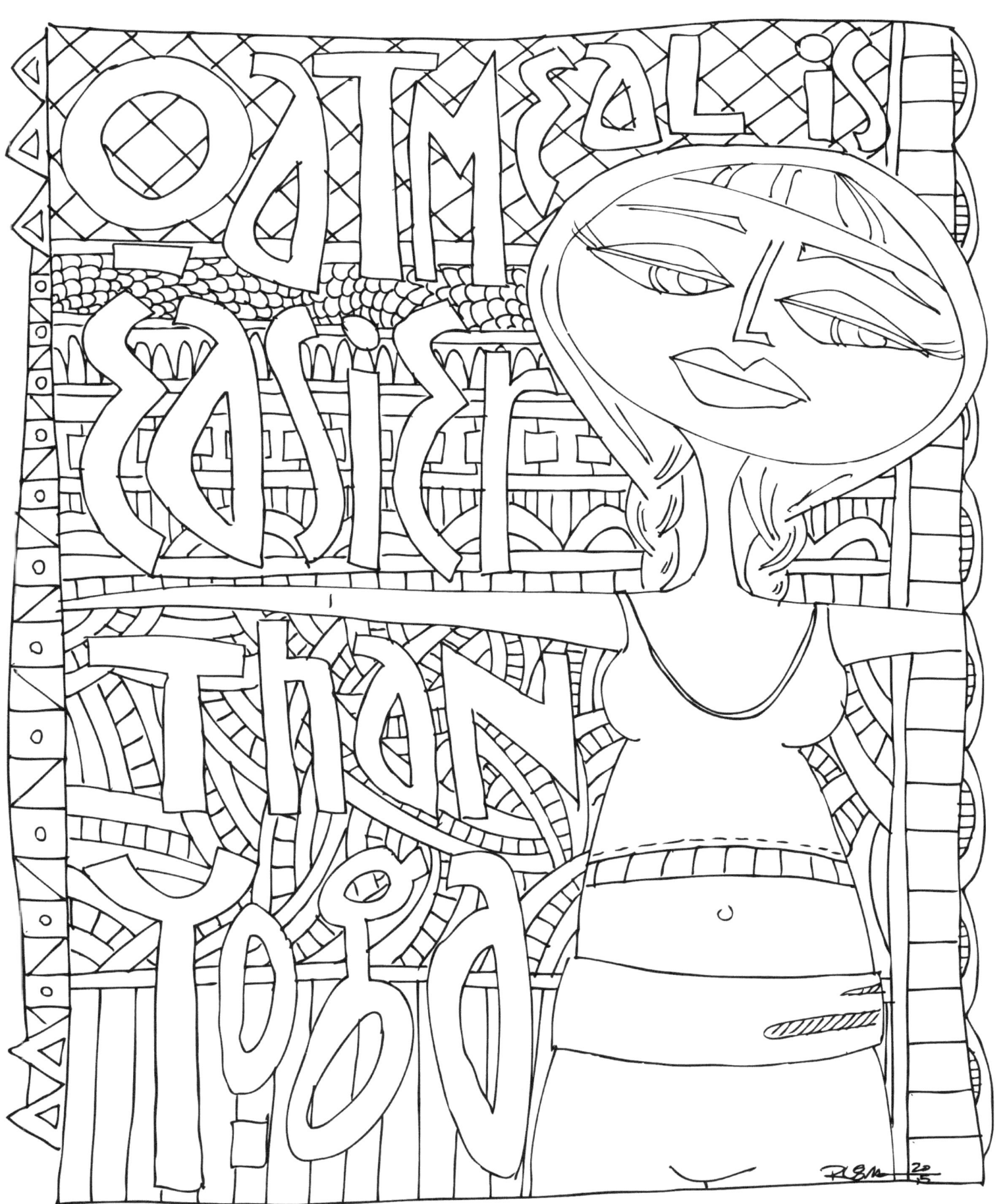

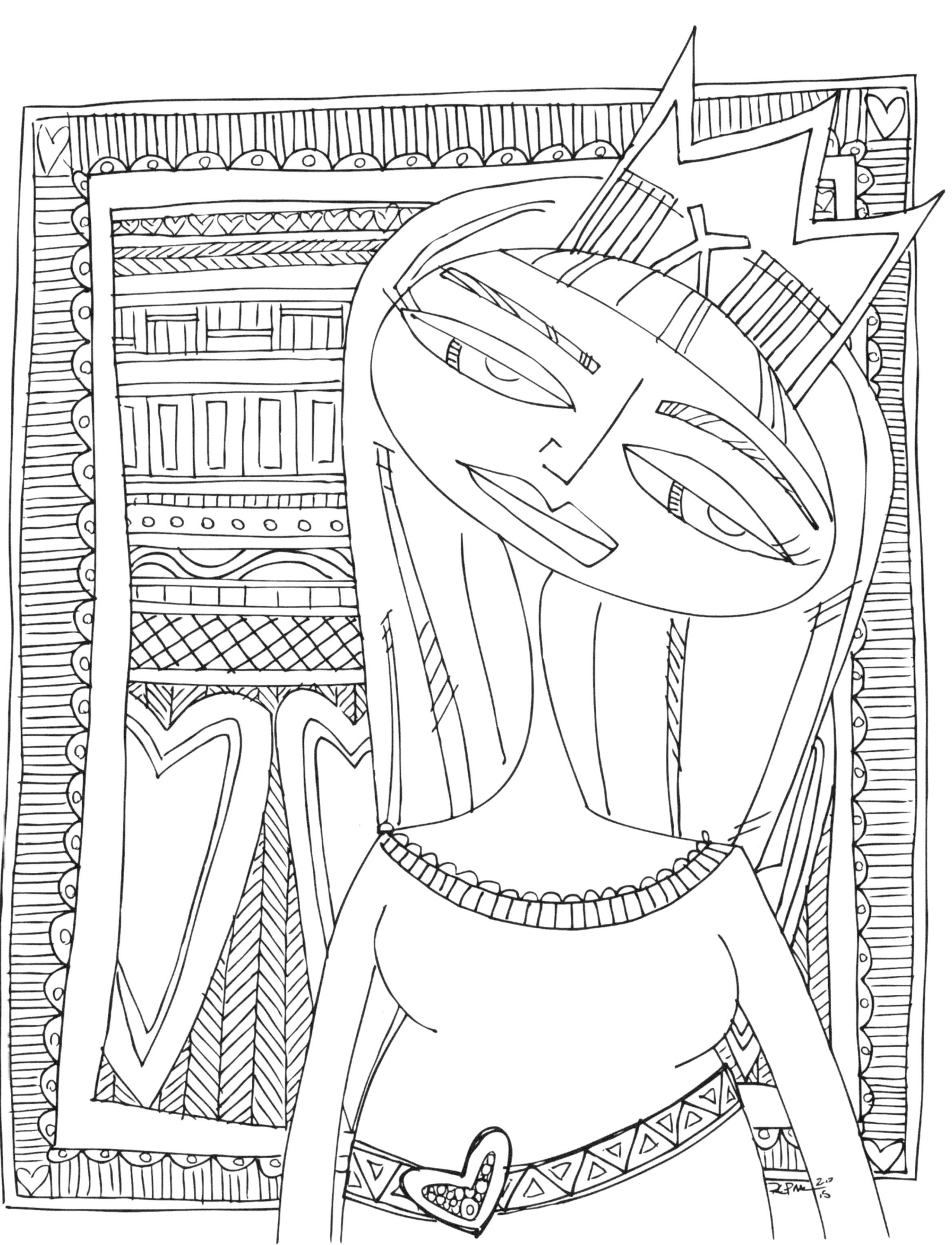

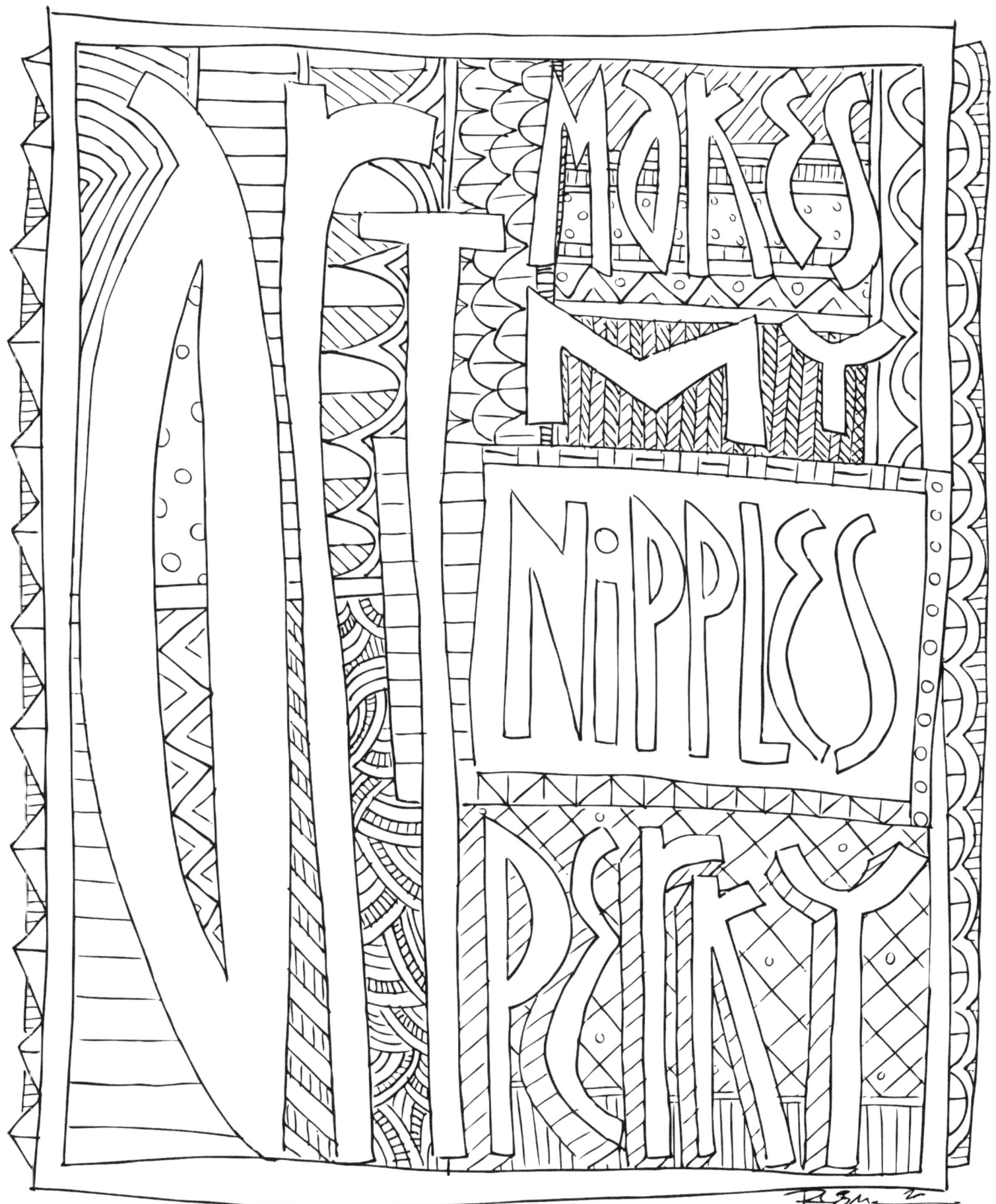

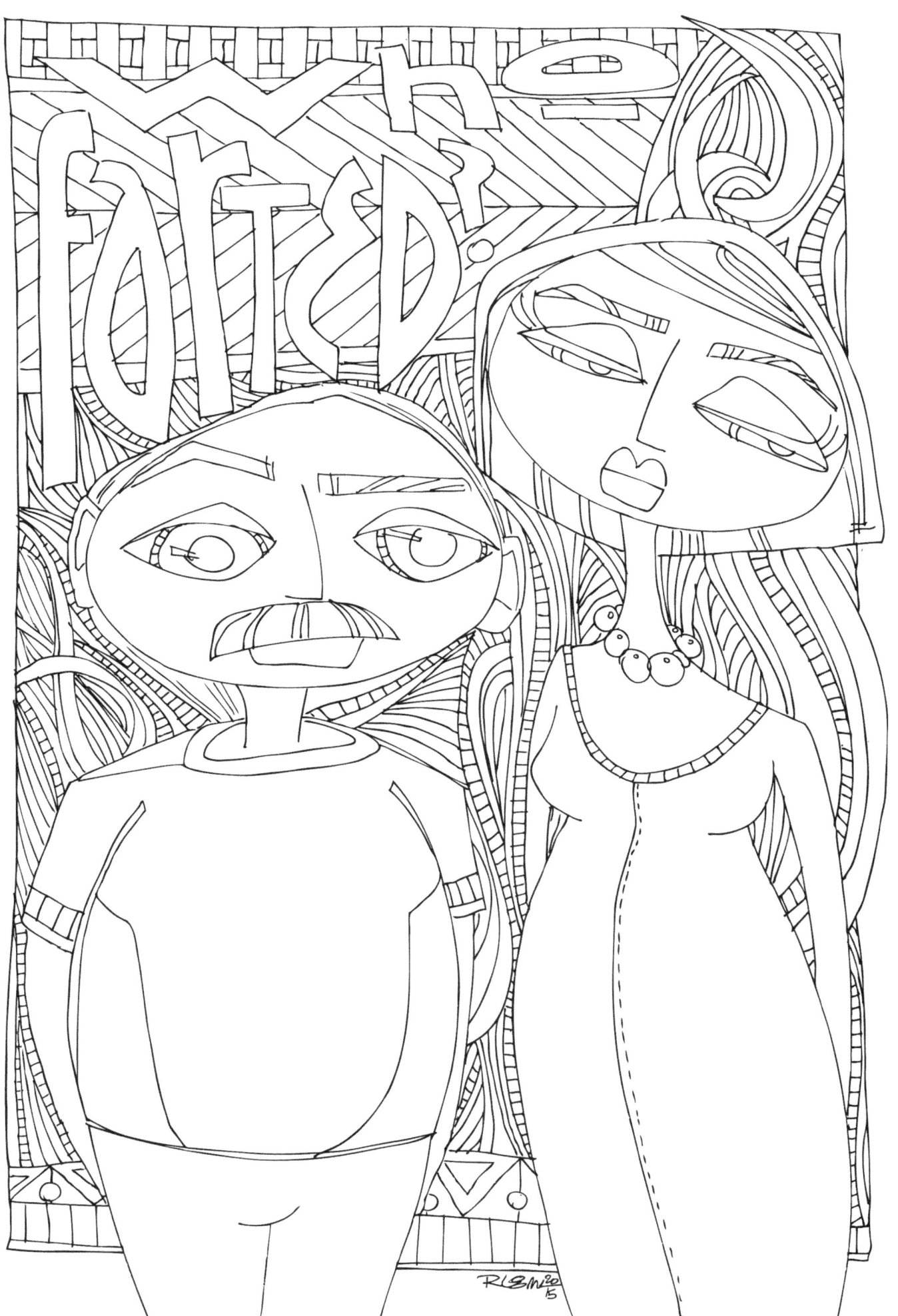

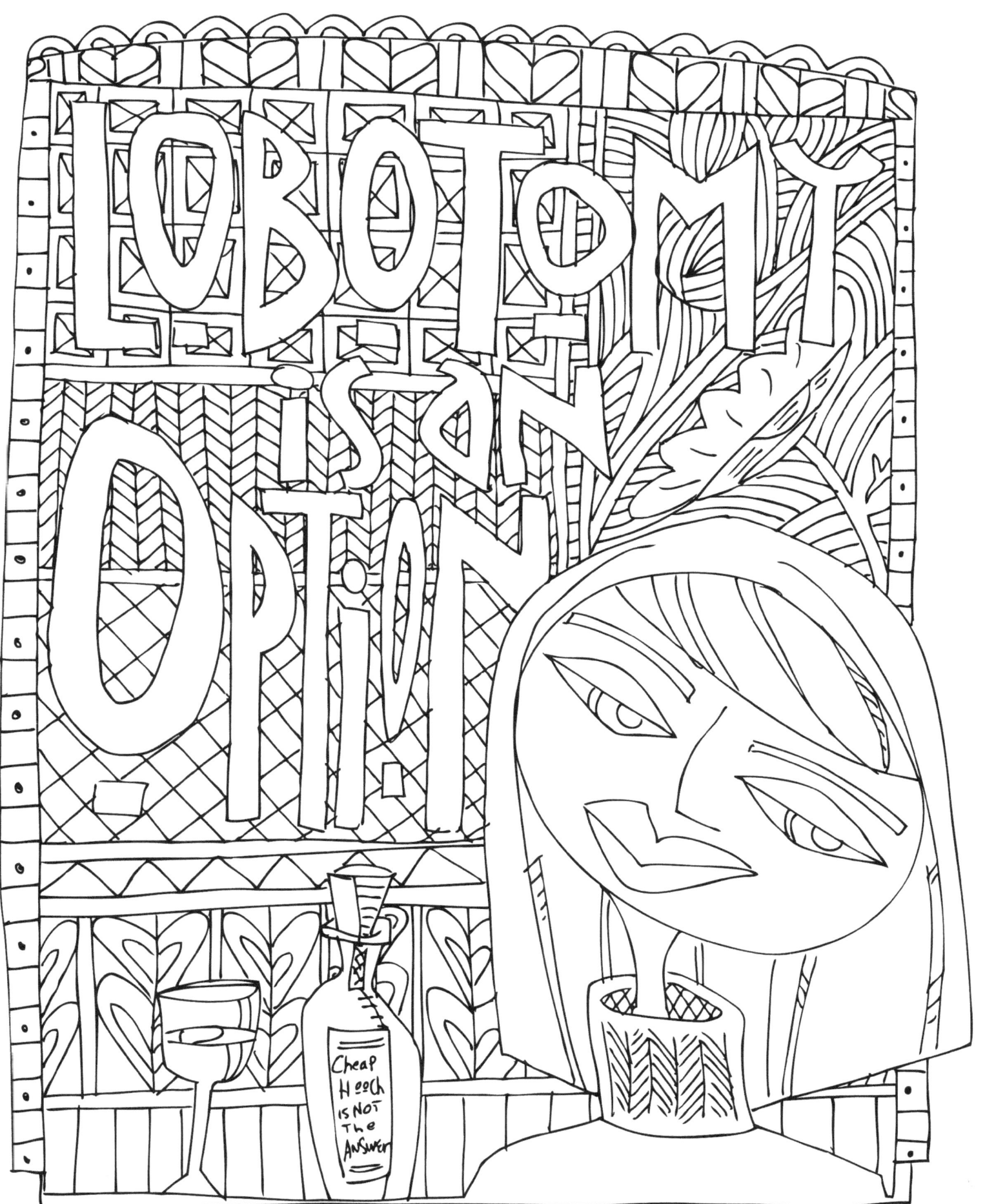

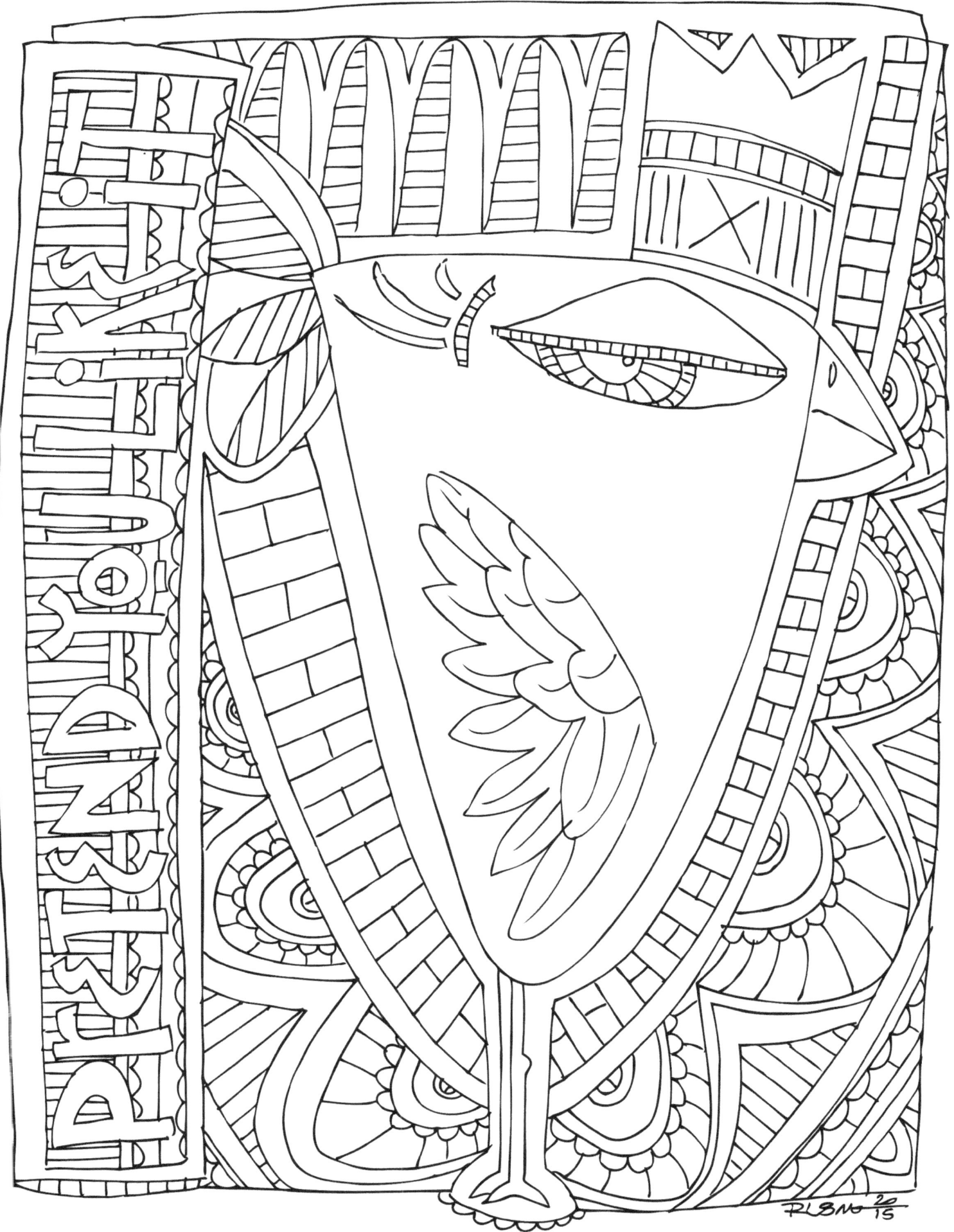

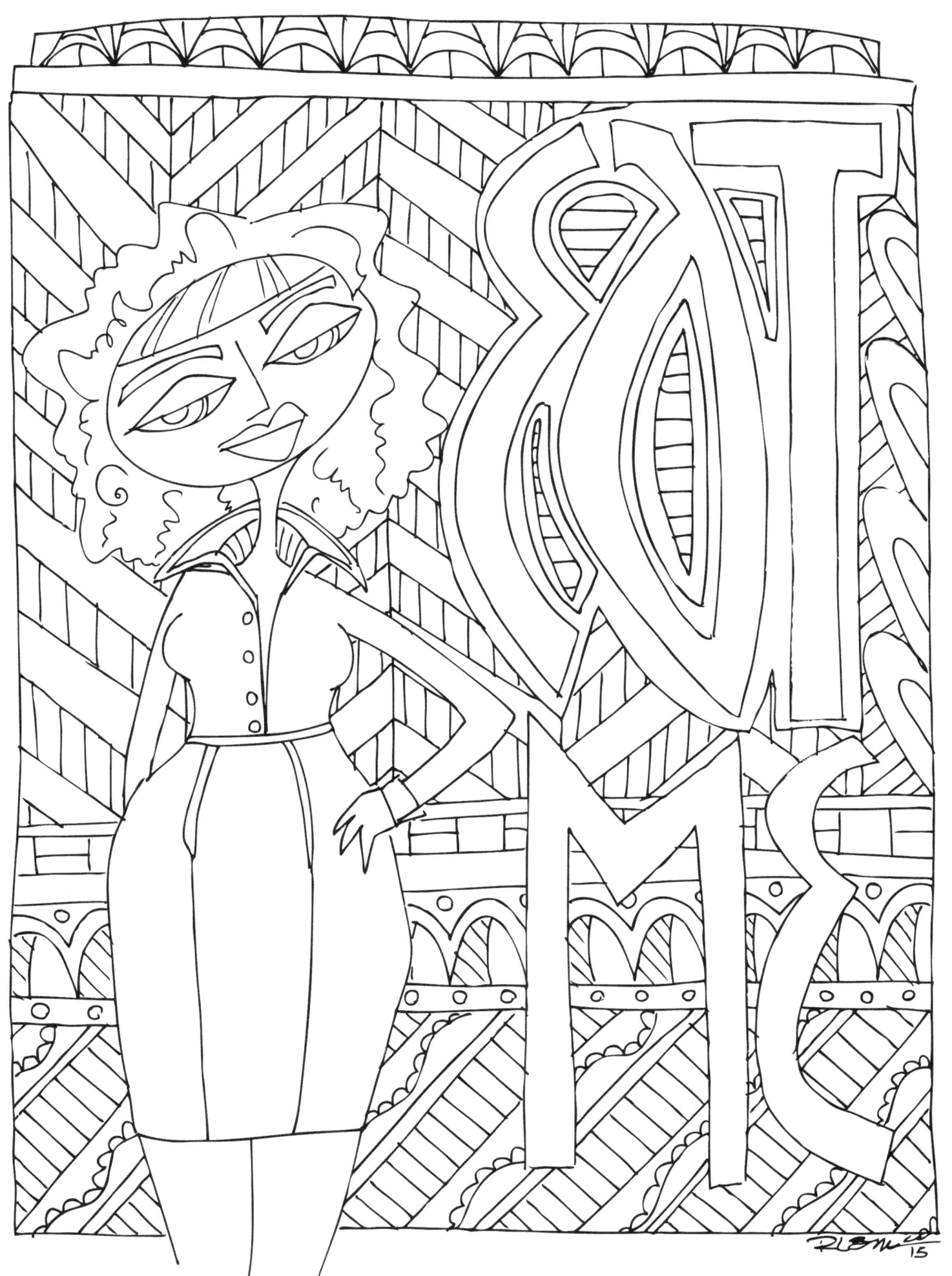

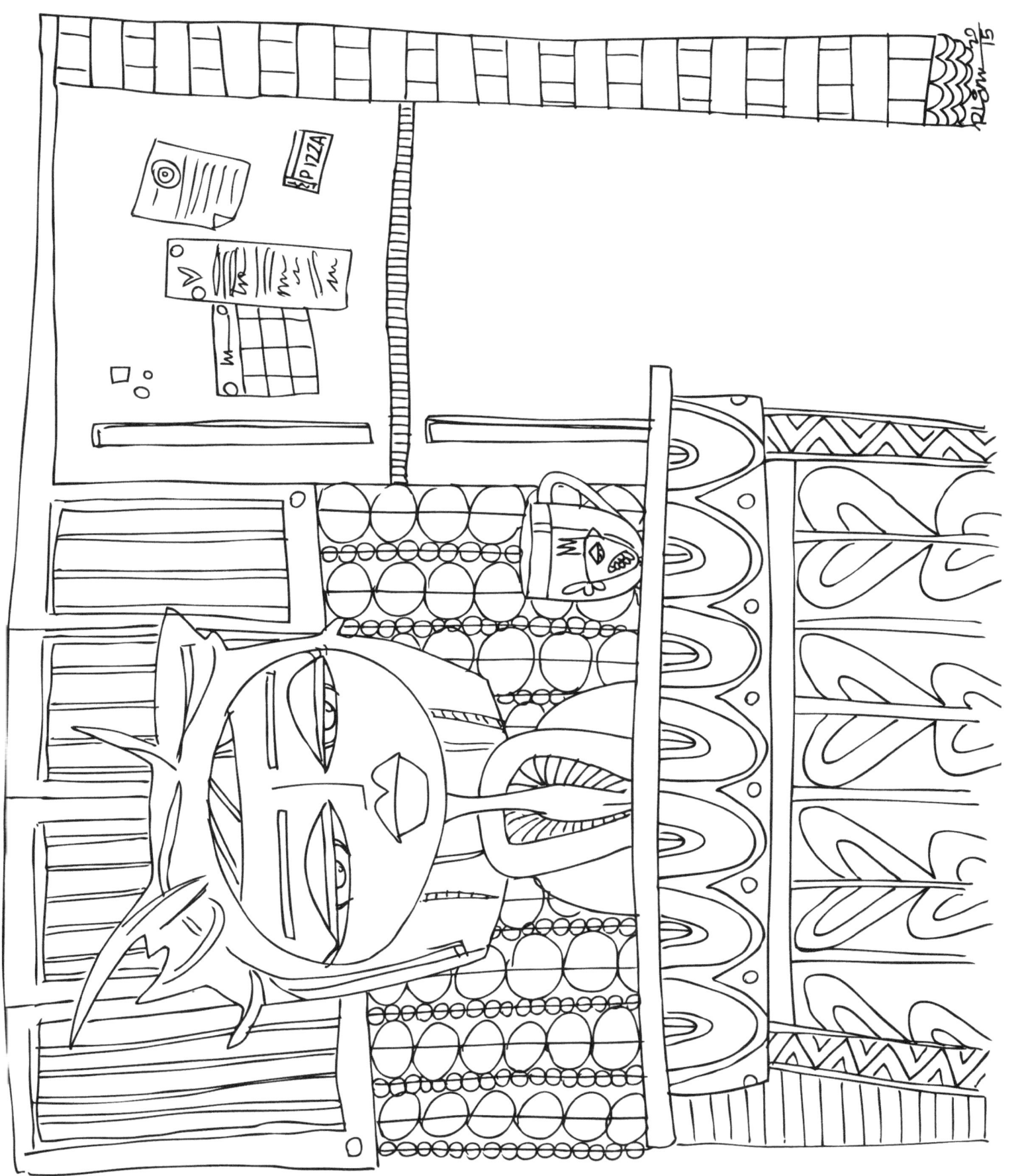

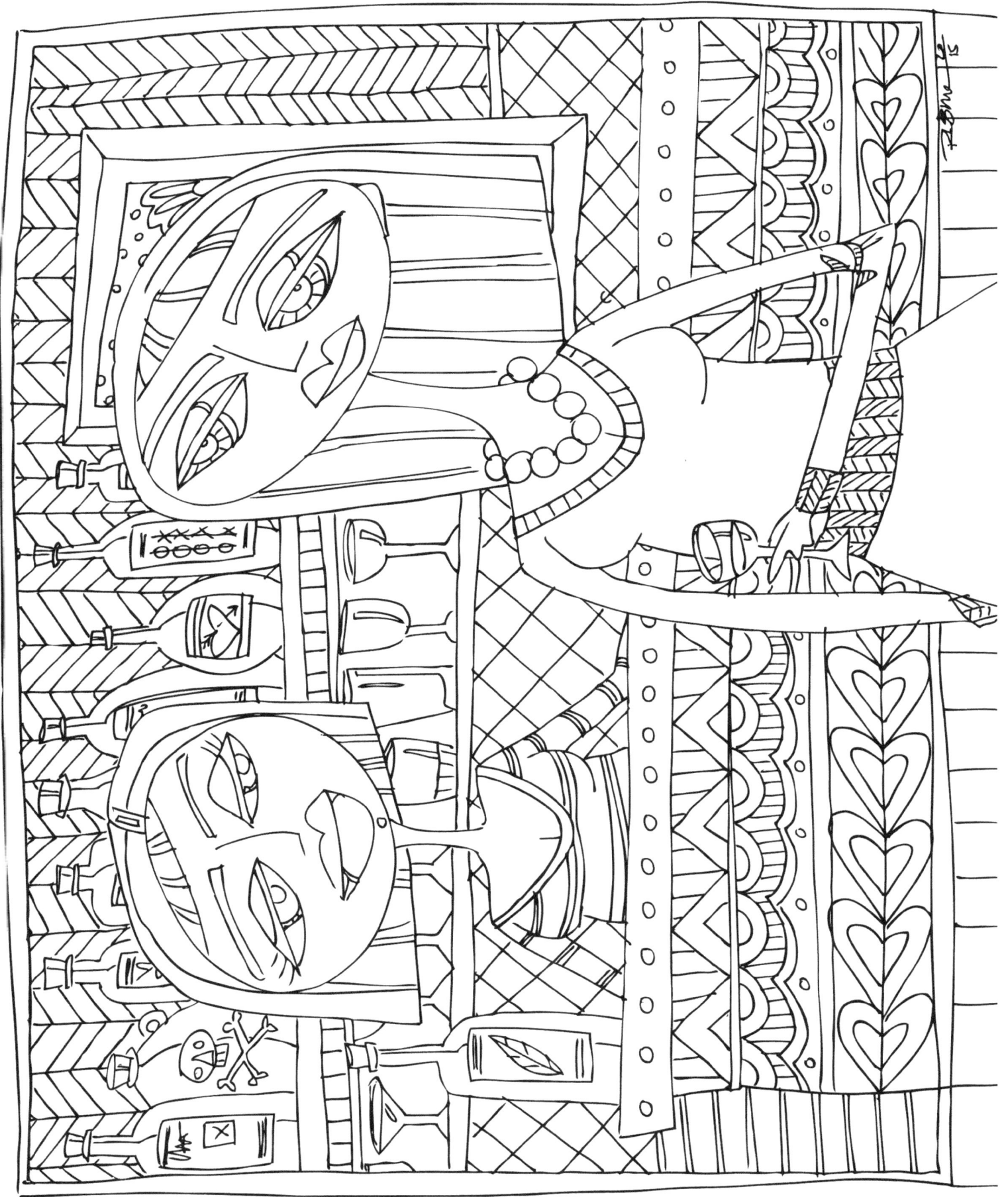

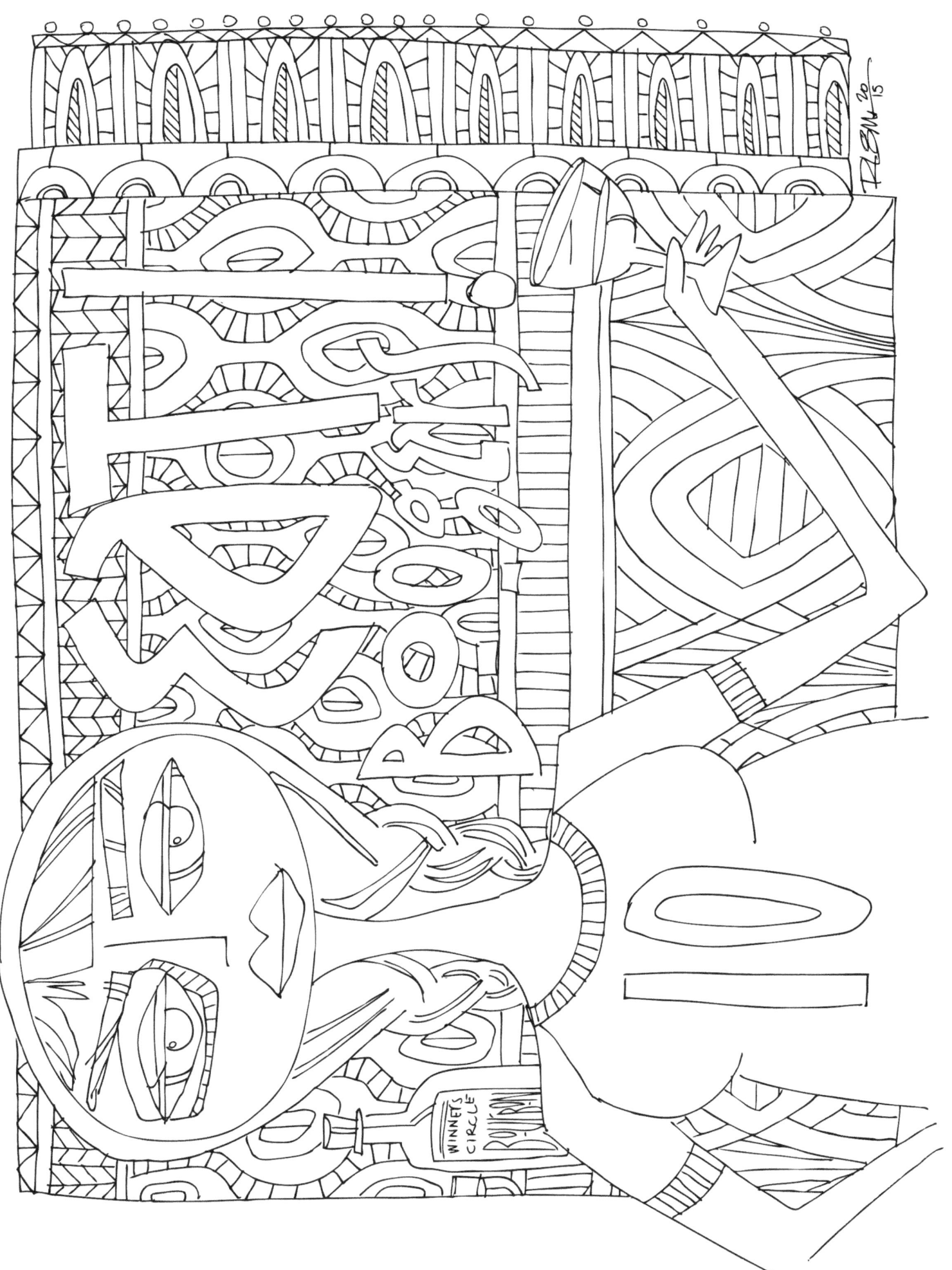

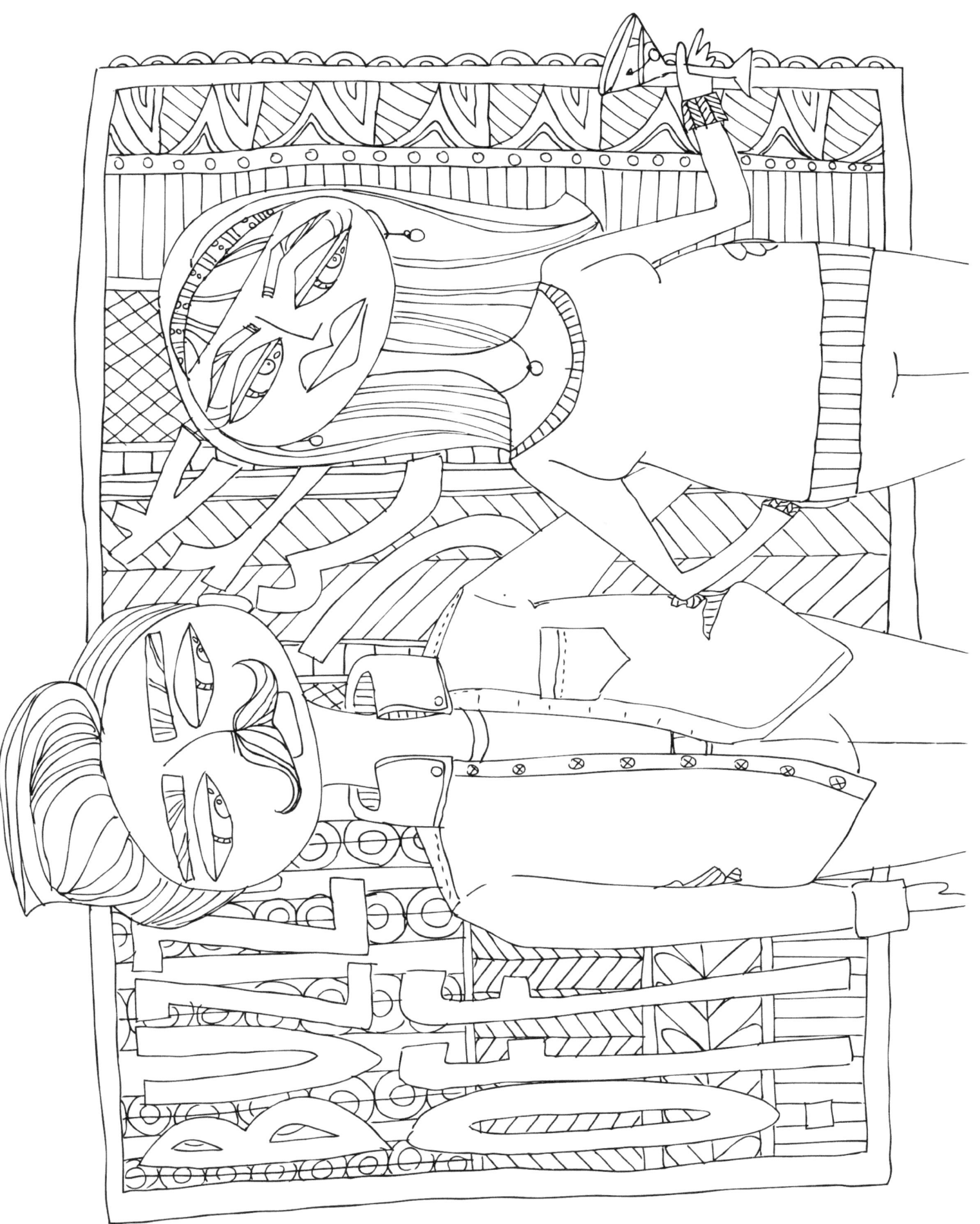

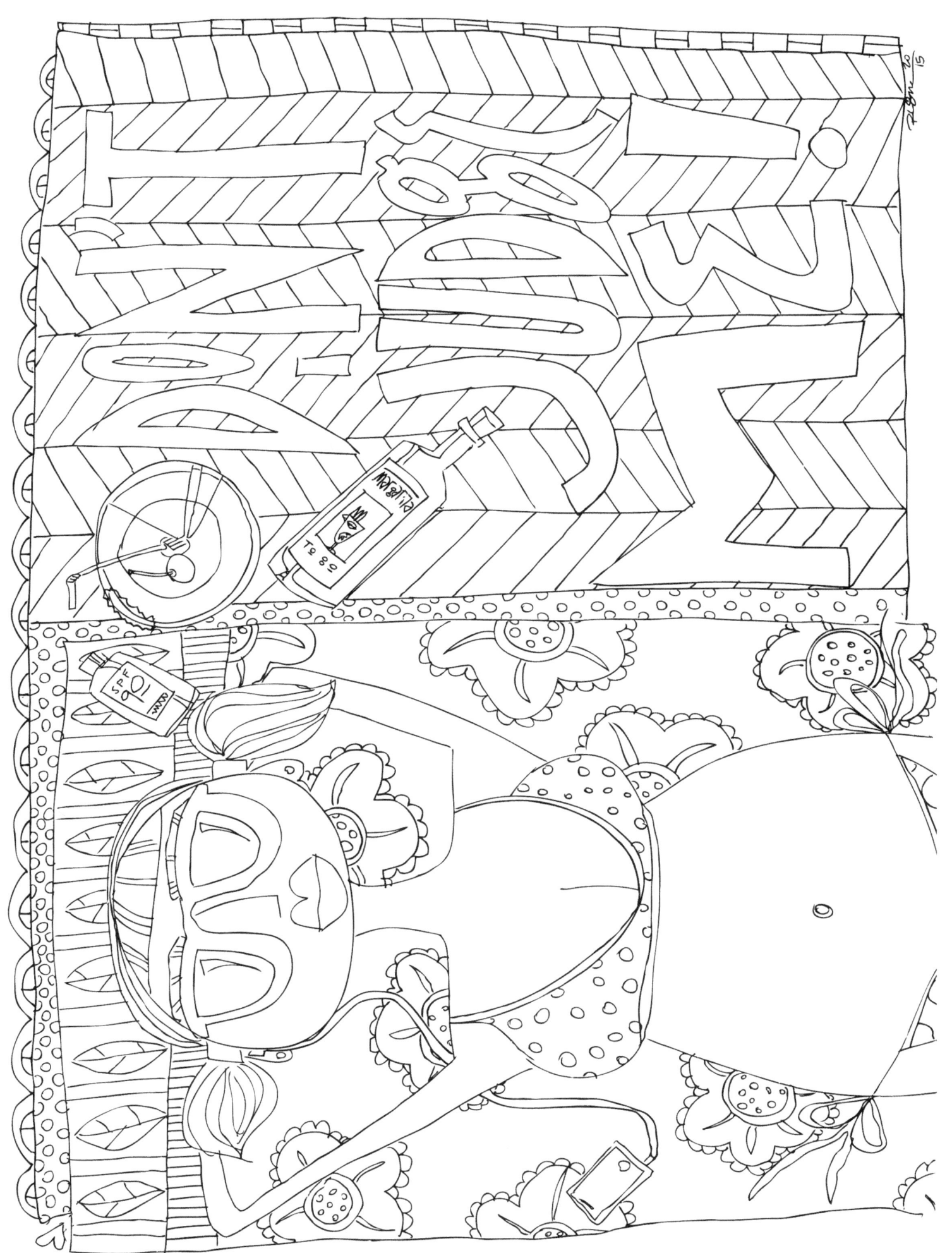

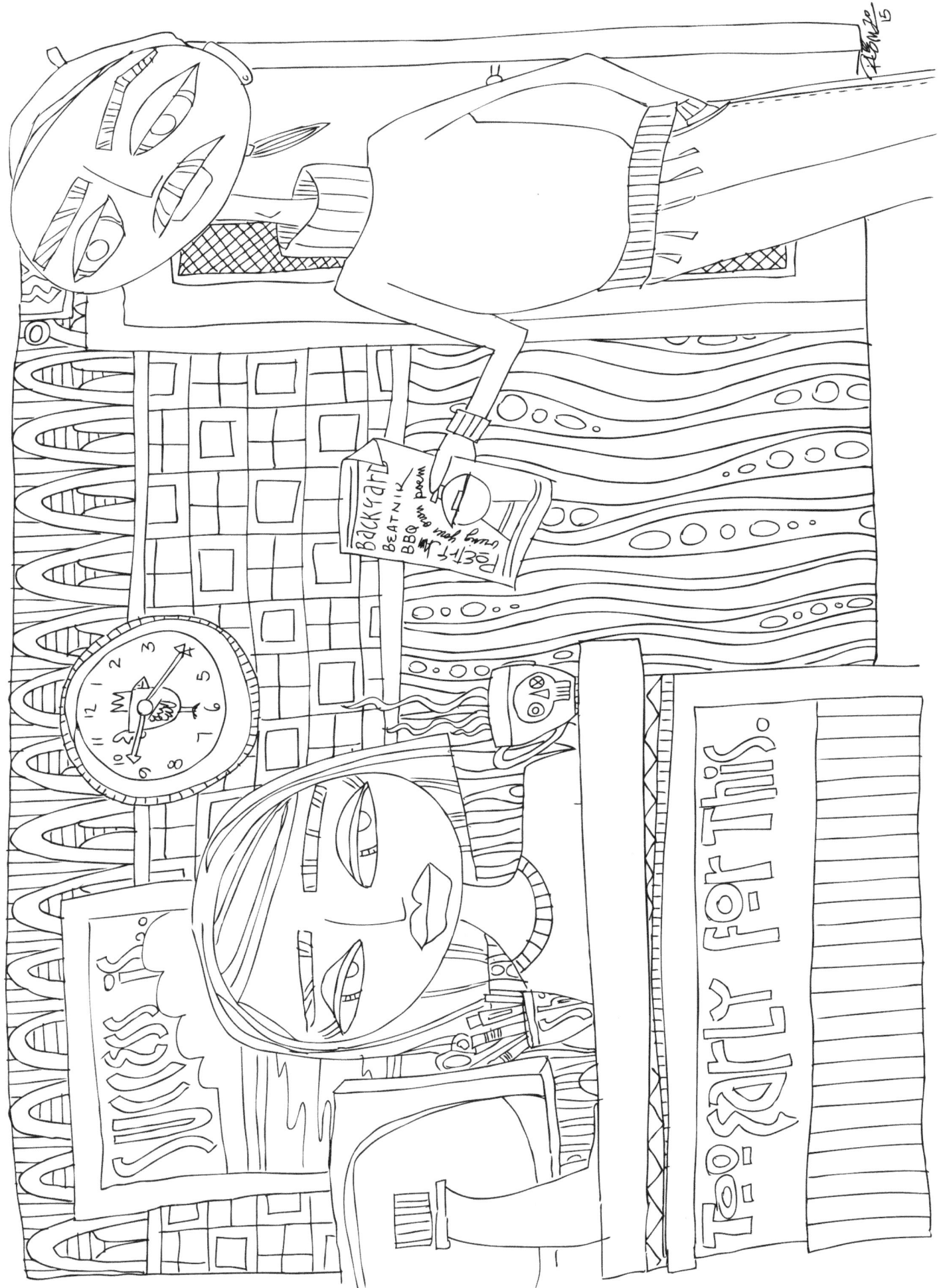

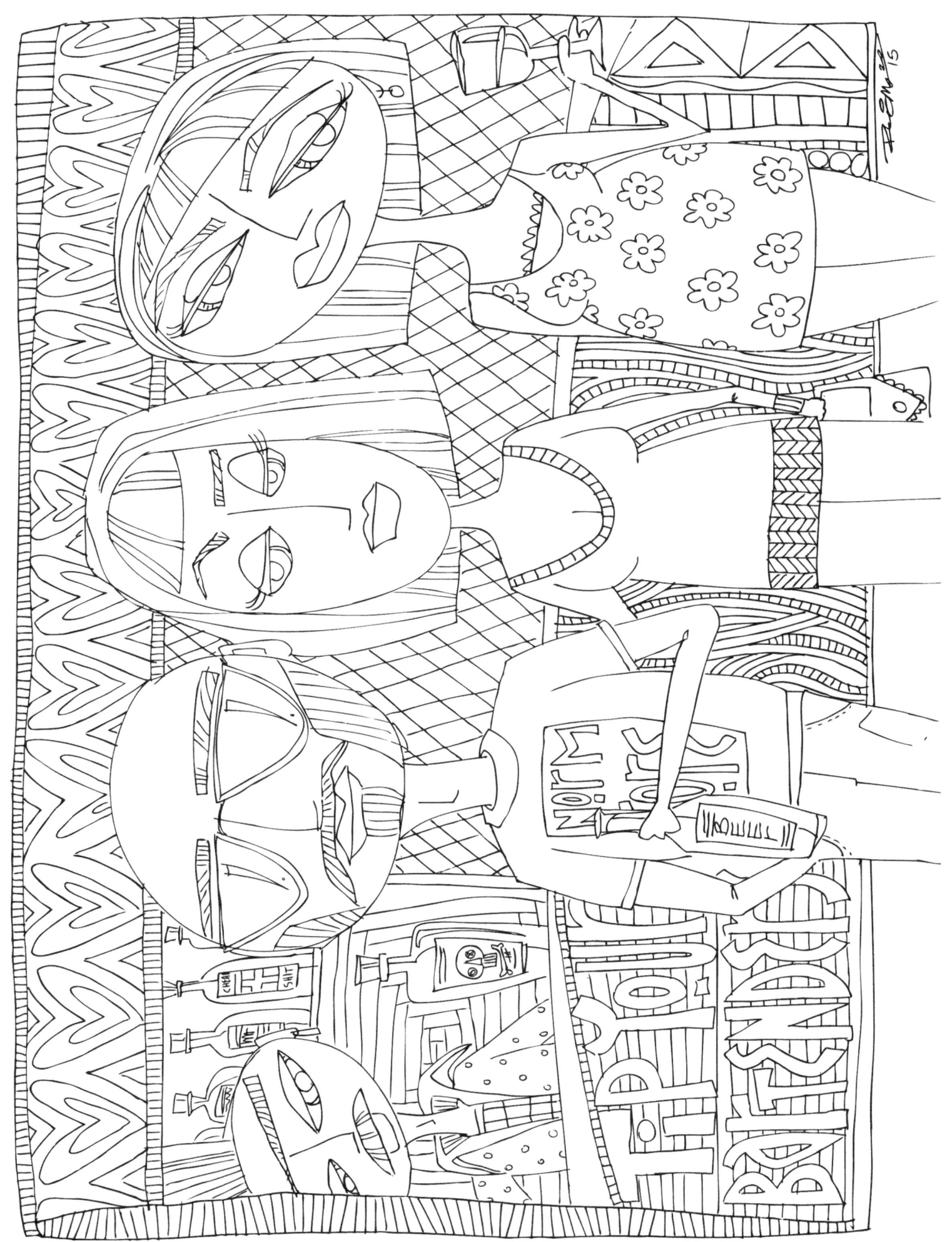

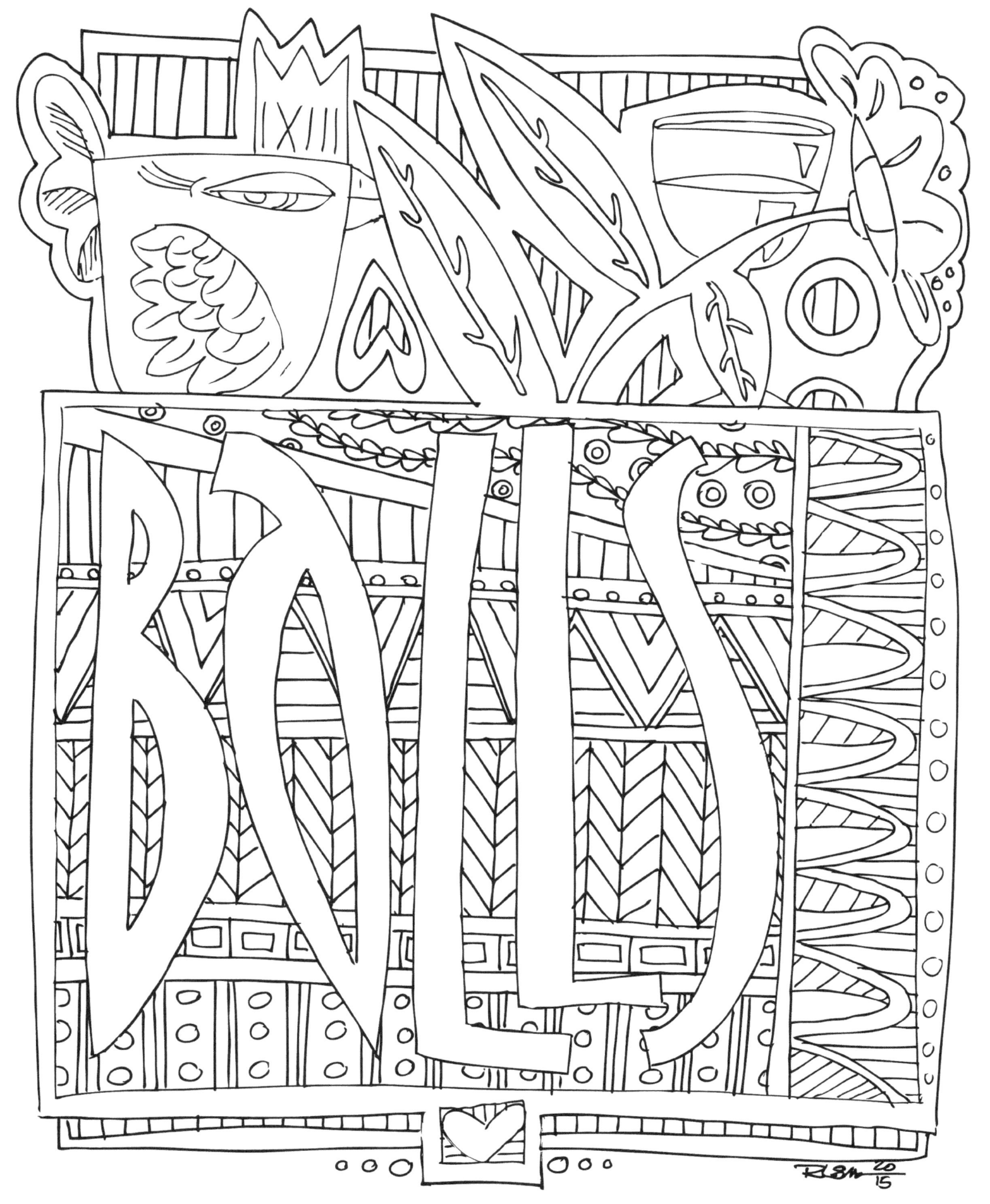

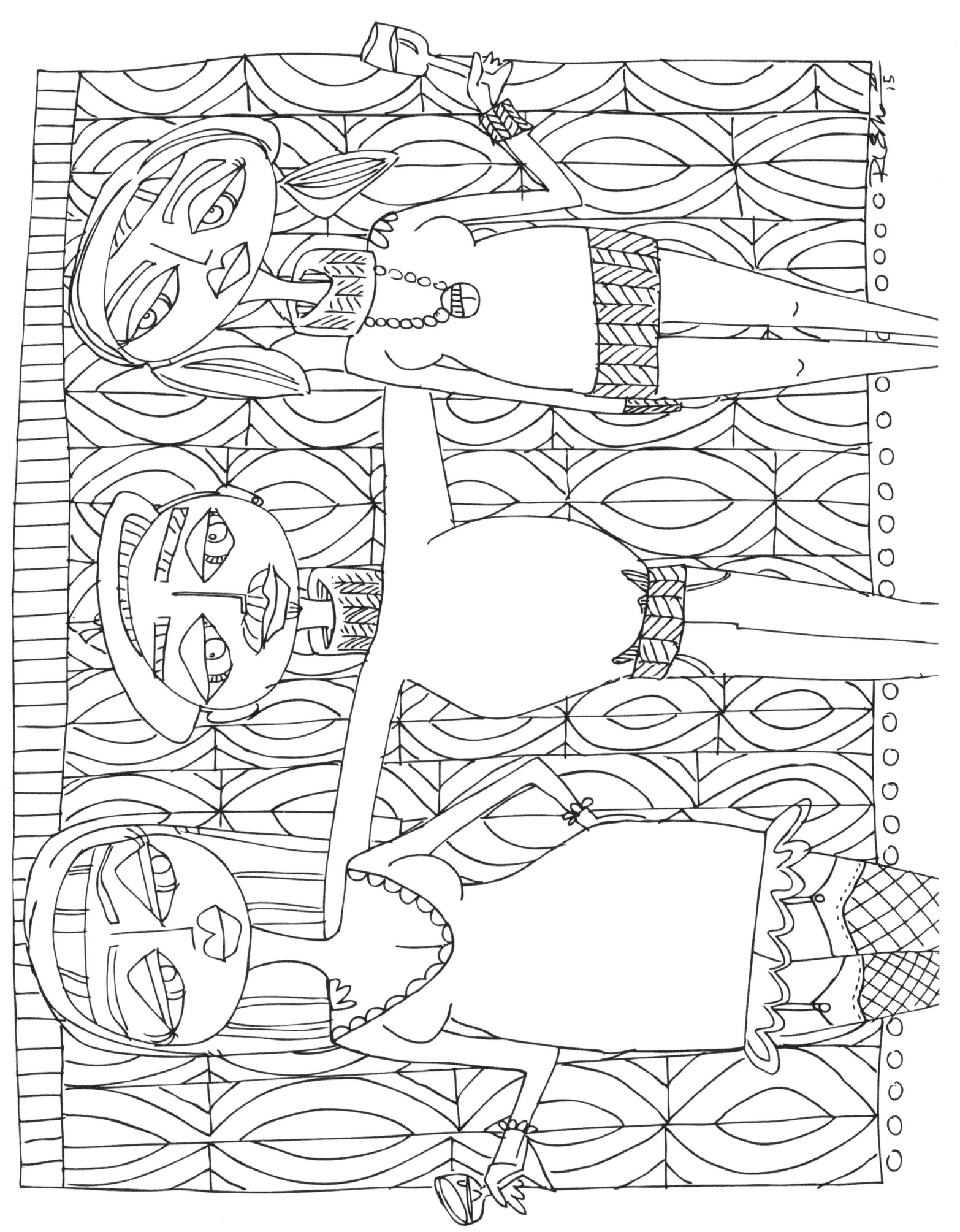